Scriabin Masterpieces
for Solo Piano
29 Works

ALEXANDER SCRIABIN

DOVER PUBLICATIONS, INC.
Mineola, New York

Bibliographical Note

This Dover edition, first published in 2001, is a new compilation of works originally published separately in authoritative early editions. The contents list, glossary and main headings are newly added. Title translations and composition dates are taken from *Scriabin: A Biography by Faubion Bowers* (Second, Revised Edition) (Dover, 1996: 0-486-28897-8).

International Standard Book Number: 0-486-41886-3

Manufactured in the United States of America
Dover Publications, Inc., 31 East 2nd Street, Mineola, N.Y. 11501

CONTENTS

GLOSSARY OF FRENCH TERMS IN THE MUSIC

Shortly after the turn of the century, Scriabin increasingly depended on the inclusion in his scores of highly original concoctions of exotic French words and phrases to capture the essence of an imagined performance. Those introduced in his *Poème languide* and later pieces are included below.

avec accablement, with pressure
avec une émotion naissante, with emerging feeling
avec une grâce dolente, with plaintive grace
avec une grâce languissante, with listless grace
avec une joie de plus en plus tumultueuse, with increasingly tumultuous joy
avec une joie voilée, with a veiled joy

comme un cri, like an outcry
comme une fanfare, like a fanfare

de plus en plus animé, more and more animated
désordonée, disordered, reckless
douloureux, déchirant, painful, heartrending

éclatant, lumineux, ringingly brilliant, luminous
envolé, taking wing
étrange, capricieusement, strange, capriciously

fier, belliqueux, ferocious, bellicose

lassé, weary
léger, light
léger onduleux, lightly swaying
lent, vague, indécis, slow, vague, unsettled

impérieux, imperiously

m.d. [*main droit*], right hand
m.g. [*main gauche*], left hand

pas vite, not fast
presto très dansant, swiftly and very dance-like

très lent, contemplatif, very slow, thoughtfully
très vite, very fast
tumultueux, tumultuous

voluptueux, charmé, voluptuous, charmed

Scriabin Masterpieces
for Solo Piano

Etude in C-sharp minor

No. 1 of *Three Pieces*, Op. 2 (1887)

Andante

Etude in F-sharp minor

No. 2 of *Twelve Etudes*, Op. 8 (1894–5)

1) *mf* (according to the composer's instructions).

2) **p**
3) _ _ _ } (according to the composer's instructions).

Etude in E major

No. 5 of *Twelve Etudes*, Op. 8 (1894–5)

1) The original tempo designation was *Allegro*. Then the composer crossed out *Allegro* in the MS and put down *Brioso*. But this later designation did not satisfy him, either; he thought later on that it did not correspond to the character of the etude.

2) *p* 〈〉 according to the composer's instructions.
3) - - - 〈〉

4) *accel.* (according to the composer's instructions).

5) In the MS and in Belyaev's edition:

6) Thus in the MS and in Belyaev's edition, but possibly this is a slip and should be: or:

7) *p*

8) *pp*   according to the composer's instructions.

9) – – –

10) - - -
11) *p*
12) - - -
13) *pp*

according to the composer's instructions.

Etude in D-sharp minor

No. 12, "Patético," of *Twelve Etudes,* Op. 8 (1894–5)

1) The MS has a *fp* here.
2) The fingering is based on the MS.

³⁾ In the MS the dynamics of the ending
are altogether different, namely:

Nocturne in D-flat major
for Left Hand Alone
No. 2 of *Two Pieces for the Left Hand Alone*, Op. 9 (1894)

SIX PRELUDES

from

Twenty-Four Preludes

Op. 11

Prelude in A minor

No. 2 (1895) of *Twenty-four Preludes*, Op. 11

1) According to the composer's instructions, a brief caesura, with following *pp*, is possible here.

2) _ _ _ (according to the composer's instructions).

1) *Accel.*
2) **pp** and *rit.* } (according to the composer's instructions).
3) See note 1.
4) See note 1.

Prelude in B minor

No. 6 (1889) of *Twenty-four Preludes,* Op. 11

Prelude in F-sharp minor

No. 8 (1896) of *Twenty-four Preludes*, Op. 11

1) Originally this *p* was not in the MS; the composer himself did not consider it obligatory and often omitted it, beginning the prelude *f*.

1) This *dim.* is not in the MS, and the composer usually did not observe it, but played *subito* **pp** in the fourth measure of this line.

2) The MS here has a ⌢ over the bar line.

3) Originally there was one more measure here, namely:

Prelude in C-sharp minor/E major

No. 9 (1894) of *Twenty-four Preludes*, Op. 11

Prelude in C-sharp minor

No. 10 (1894) of *Twenty-four Preludes*, Op. 11

Prelude in E-flat minor

No. 14 (1895) of *Twenty-four Preludes*, Op. 11

1) In the MS:

2) In the MS and in Belyaev's edition:

3) accel.
4) ten. } according to the composer's instructions.

Fantaisie in B minor

Op. 28 (1900–01)

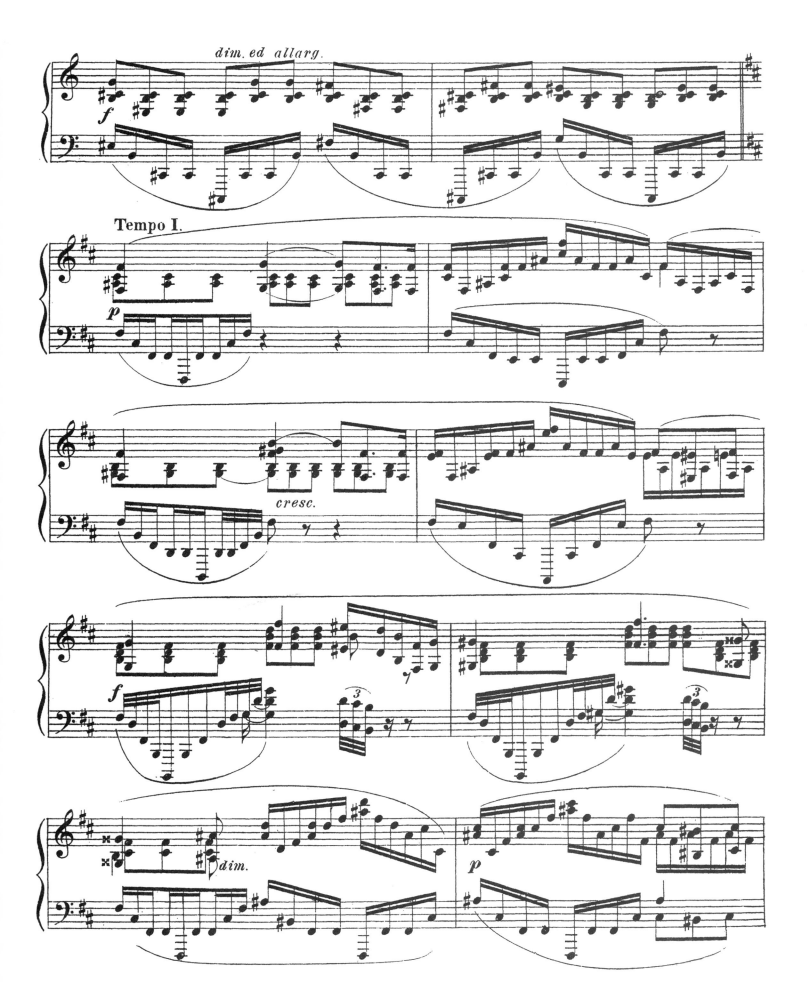

Poème in F-sharp major

No. 1 of *Two Poems*, Op. 32 (1903)

Poème satanique

"Satanic poem" / Op. 36 (1903)

Etude in C-sharp minor

No. 5 of *Eight Etudes*, Op. 42 (1903)

Danse languide

"Dance of languor"/No. 4 of *Four Pieces,* Op. 51 (1906)

Poème languide

"Poem of languor"/No. 3 of *Three Pieces*, Op. 52 (1905–07)

Enigme

"Enigma"/No. 2 of *Three Pieces,* Op. 52 (1905–07)

Sonata No. 5
in F-sharp major
Op. 53 (1907)

„Я к жизни призываю вас, скрытые стремленья!„
„Вы, утонувшие в темных глубинах
Духа творящего, вы, боязливые
Жизни зародыши, вам дерзновенье я приношу.„

(Поэми экстизи, стр. 11)

"I summon you to life, secret yearnings!
You who have been drowned in the dark depths
Of the creative spirit, you timorous
Embryos of life, it is to you that I bring daring."

(Poem of Ecstasy, 11)

68

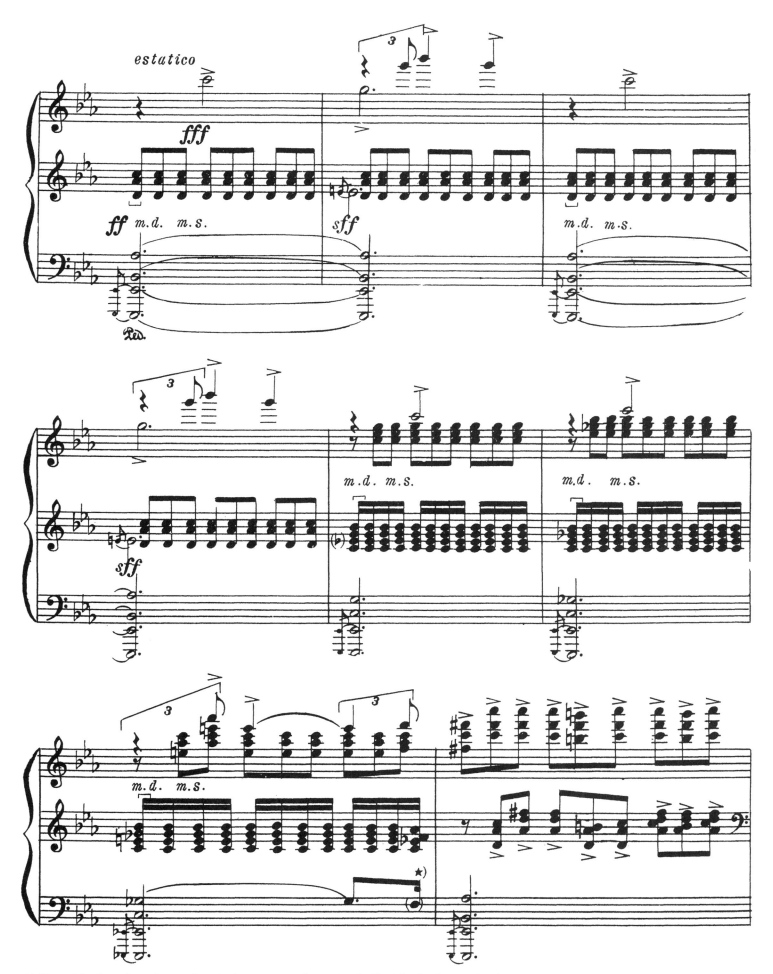

*) If need be [OR, Strictly speaking], this note can be omitted. (Scriabin's observation.)

Désir

"Desire"/No. 1 of *Two Pieces,* Op. 57 (1908)

Caresse dansée

"Danced caress"/No. 2 of *Two Pieces*, Op. 57 (1908)

Vers la flamme: Poème

"Poem, Toward the flame"/Op. 72 (1914)

Guirlandes

"Garlands" / No. 1 of *Two Dances*, Op. 73 (1914)

[*Two Dances* are passages from Scriabin's unfinished *Mysterium*. They are among his final works, composed in the spring of 1914.]

Flammes sombres

"Dark Flames"/No. 2 of *Two Dances*, Op. 73 (1914)

[*Two Dances* are passages from Scriabin's unfinished *Mysterium*. They are among his final works, composed in the spring of 1914.]

Presto très dansant.

FIVE [Last] PRELUDES
Op. 74 (1914)
Prelude No. 1

Douloureux, déchirant

Prelude No. 2

From *Five [Last] Preludes*, Op. 74 (1914)

Très lent, contemplatif

Prelude No. 3

From *Five [Last] Preludes*, Op. 74 (1914)

Prelude No. 4

From *Five [Last] Preludes,* Op. 74 (1914)

Prelude No. 5

From *Five [Last] Preludes*, Op. 74 (1914)

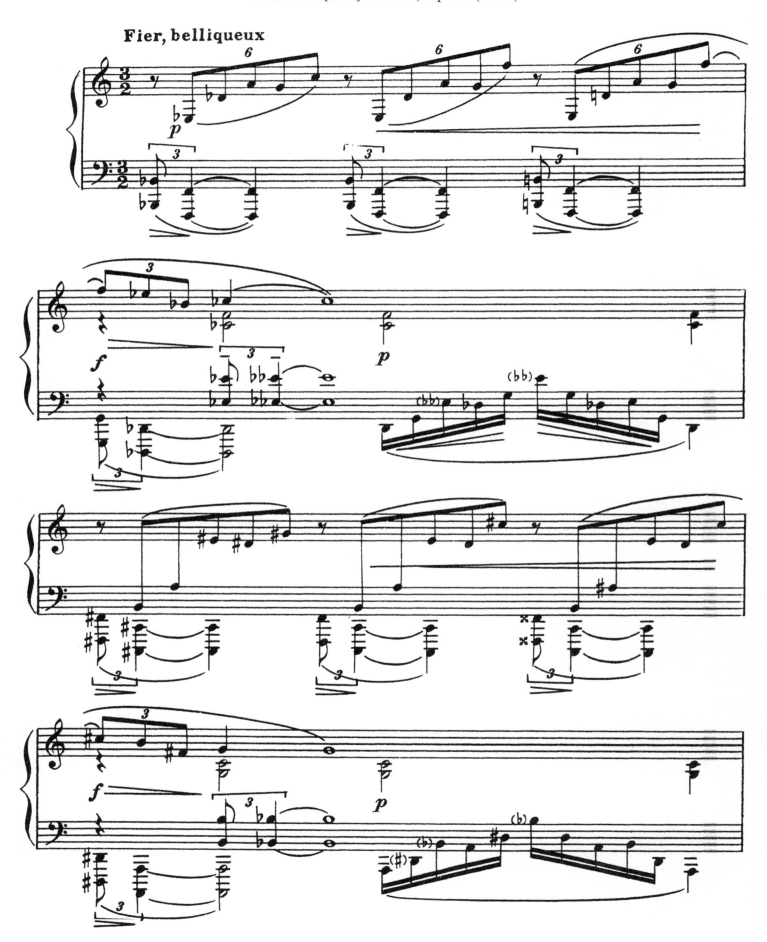